Musicians

Leslie Strudwick

Crabtree Publishing Company

Dedication

This series is dedicated to every woman who has followed her dreams and to every young girl who hopes to do the same. While overcoming great odds and often oppression, the remarkable women in this series have triumphed in their fields. Their dedication, hard work, and excellence can serve as an inspiration to all—young and old, male and female. Women in Profile is both an acknowledgment of and a tribute to these great women.

Project Manager
Lauri Seidlitz
Crabtree Editor
Virginia Mainprize
Copy Editor
Krista McLuskey
Design and Layout
Warren Clark

Published by Crabtree Publishing Company

350 Fifth Avenue, Suite 3308
New York, NY
USA 10018

360 York Road, R.R. 4
Niagara-on-the-Lake
Ontario, Canada
L0S 1J0

Copyright © 1998 WEIGL EDUCATIONAL PUBLISHERS LIMITED. All rights reserved. No part of this publication may be reproduced, stored in a retrieval system or be transmitted in any form or by any means, electronic, mechanical, photocopying, recording, or otherwise, without the prior written permission of Weigl Educational Publishers Limited.

Cataloging-in-Publication Data

Strudwick, Leslie 1970–
      Musicians / Leslie Strudwick.
          p. cm. — (Women in Profile)
      Includes bibliographical references and index.
      Summary: Chronicles the lives and achievements of noted female musicians, including jazz pianist and composer Lil Hardin Armstrong, violinist Midori, and harpsichordist Wanda Landowska.
      ISBN 0-7787-0009-7 (rlb). — ISBN 0-7787-0031-3 (pbk.)
      1. Women musicians—Biography—Juvenile literature. [1. Women musicians. 2. Musicians. 3. Women—Biography.] I. Title. II. Series
ML3929.S77   1998
780'.92'2—dc21
[B]
          98-10990
          CIP
          AC MN

Photograph Credits

Every reasonable effort has been made to trace ownership and to obtain permission to reprint copyright material. The publishers would be pleased to have any errors or omissions brought to their attention so that they may be corrected in subsequent printings. Archive Photos: pages 36, 37, 38, 40 (Frank Driggs), 25, 29; BMG Music: page 43; Courtesy of Liona Boyd: pages 9 (David Falconer), 10 (Keith Williamson), 6, 7, 8, 11; Canapress Photo Service: pages 18, 21; Corbis: page 35 (Robert Spencer); Culver Pictures, Inc.: page 39; Duke University: page 41; Edinburgh International Festival: page 22; Globe and Mail: page 20; Globe Photos: cover, pages 32 (Stephen Trupp), 33 (John Barrett), 34 (Richard Chambury); ICM Artists: pages 12, 13 (Brigitte Lacombe); Muse Records: page 42; National Portrait Gallery: page 24 (John Singer Sargent); Nigel Nicolson: page 28; NYC Records: page 45; Walter H. Scott: pages 14, 15, 16, 17; Topham Picture Point: pages 30 (David Giles), 23, 26, 27; Warner Music Canada: page 44.

Contents

More Women in Profile

Musicians

M usic is sound that is arranged into pleasing and interesting patterns. Music is important in every culture and every country around the world. Many people use music to express their feelings and ideas. Many more use music for entertainment and enjoyment.

Musicians are people who are trained in music. They may earn their living by playing, singing, composing, or conducting music. This book will introduce you to women with a wide range of musical talents.

Some of the women in this book became musicians at a time when few women entered the field. Until the last two hundred years or so, only the flute and the harp were considered appropriate instruments for women. All others were believed to be too unladylike.

Women musicians of the twentieth century have changed these ideas with their lives and work. Today, there are many successful women players, singers, composers, and conductors. Women work in all styles of music, including jazz, classical, and pop. Some have created new styles of music by combining sounds in different ways.

One book could not include all the respected women musicians from around the world. The women profiled in this volume come from many countries and backgrounds. They have contributed to the world of music in many different ways. As you read, you may think of other musicians whose work inspires you.

"Music contributes profoundly to the richness and beauty of life. I feel so fortunate to be able to share this wonderful international language with people around the world."

Liona Boyd

Canadian Guitarist

Early Years

Born in London, England, Liona moved with her family to Canada when she was six years old. She gave her first recital on the ship crossing the ocean. She played the **recorder** in a talent competition.

Liona was given her first guitar as a Christmas present when she was fourteen. Her parents had brought it back from a trip to Spain when she was four or five. Liona practiced fifteen to twenty minutes each day at her mother's urging. After Liona's mother took her to a concert performed by Julian Bream, a famous English guitarist, Liona was inspired. She began to practice one to two hours a day on her own.

When Liona's family moved to Mexico for a year, Liona's teacher sent her music so that she could practice by herself. She started to love Spanish music.

BACKGROUNDER

The Guitar

The guitar was first developed in Egypt about five thousand years ago. The instrument became popular in Europe around three thousand years later. The guitar has seen many changes from when it was first developed. The modern guitar was made around the late 1800s. There are two types of guitars today, the **acoustic** and the electric. Liona plays an acoustic guitar.

Two-year-old Liona with her teddy bear Moses.

Developing Skills

Liona graduated with honors from high school. Then, she enrolled in the music program at the University of Toronto in Ontario, Canada. In 1972, Liona earned her Bachelor of Music degree in Performance and graduated with honors. The same year, she also won the Canadian National Music Competition.

Wanting to see more of the world, Liona moved to Paris, France. There she studied for two years with one of the world's top guitarists, Alexandre Lagoya. She studied for six to seven hours each day. He was pleased with his new pupil and called her "one of my most brilliant students."

In 1975, Liona returned to Canada and recorded her first album, *The Guitar*. This album introduced her to the world as one of the greatest guitarists of her time. She did her first major tour of Canada and then went to New York City to make her **debut** at Carnegie Hall. Her life of touring the world had begun.

After her debut at Carnegie Hall, The New York Times *praised Liona's "flair for brilliance."*

Liona was devoted to music. She released two more albums in just two years. She also appeared on several television specials, performed with orchestras, and toured Latin America. She visited Peru, Colombia, Venezuela, and Brazil. Guitar music is very popular in these countries, and many of the songs that Liona played there were written by Latin-American composers.

Liona continued to record a new album each year. In 1978, she released *The First Lady of the Guitar* which won Canadian music awards and more fans for Liona's music. One of Liona's favorite songs on this album was written especially for her by composer Milton Barnes. The piece, called "Fantasy for Guitar," is based on the North American aboriginal folk song called "Land of the Silver Birch." It is a musical picture of the forests and lakes of Northern Canada. Some of the sounds are made by hitting the guitar strings and by rapping on the body of the guitar. These sounds copy those you might hear in the wilderness.

Liona practices three to four hours each day. She does scales and technical exercises while watching the news on television.

"I like to play my own pieces and share the emotion."

Liona has performed for the British royal family, the presidents of the United States and Mexico, and the prime ministers of Canada, France, and Britain.

Accomplishments

Liona wanted to play more than just classical guitar. She teamed up with many musicians to tour and record songs. She toured with folk singer Gordon Lightfoot and played to sold-out theaters across Canada and the United States. Liona also tried country music. She went to Nashville in 1979 and played with the country music star Chet Atkins.

Liona wanted to challenge herself further. In 1984, after playing in a series of concerts in Asia, she took a short break from touring to compose more of her own music. She also published a music book called *Favorite Solos for Classical Guitar*.

In 1985, many musicians from around the world got together to record songs to raise money for Ethiopia, an African country. Ethiopia was suffering from war and **drought**. Millions of people were starving to death. British musicians led the way with their song "Do They Know It's Christmas?" American musicians raised money with a song called "We Are the World." Liona was part of a group of Canadian musicians who also wanted to help. They recorded the song "Tears Are Not Enough."

Because of her experiments with folk, rock, and pop music, Liona has brought many new listeners to classical music. However, some people think she should concentrate on classical music. Liona disagrees. She has an adventurous spirit and wants to try new things. She thinks that trying new musical styles has made her a better musician.

Liona is most proud of one her latest albums, *Classically Yours.* She composed every song on the recording. Liona had noticed that people at concerts enjoyed her original work. Although many classical performers do not compose their own music, Liona wanted to perform her own pieces. She believes composing, recording, and performing her own music makes her work unique in the world of classical guitar.

"I enjoy some of the interesting experiences I've had. I don't believe classical artists have to be so mysterious."

Quick Notes

- Liona's **autobiography**, called *With Strings Attached,* was published in 1998.

- Beside her wall of awards and photos, Liona has a section devoted to her cat, Muffin.

- Liona likes to paint in her spare time.

Liona and her cat, Muffin.
Liona supports many animal rights groups. She often gives concerts to raise money for causes involving animals.

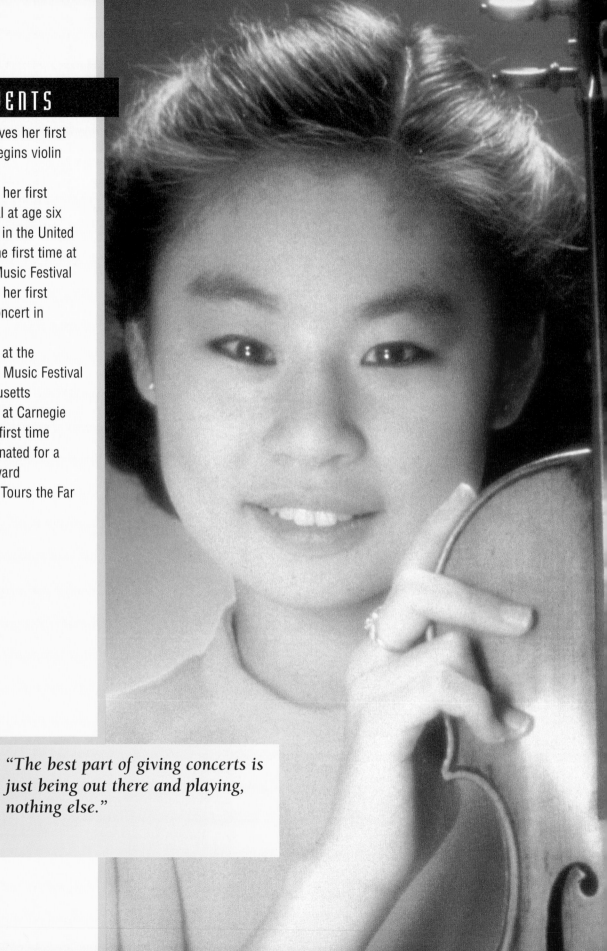

"The best part of giving concerts is just being out there and playing, nothing else."

Midori

Japanese Violinist

Early Years

Midori Goto was born an only child in Osaka, Japan. Her father was an engineer and her mother was a professional violinist. Midori's mother, Setsu Goto, said that "almost from the moment Midori was born, I knew she was sensitive to music."

When she went to the concert hall to rehearse, Midori's mother took her baby daughter along. Midori often napped in the front row while her mother practiced on stage. One day, when Midori was just two years old, she began humming the piece of music that her mother had practiced two days before.

Midori was fascinated by her mother's violin. The violin was kept on top of the family piano, and Midori often tried to climb on the piano to reach it. On her third birthday, Midori was given her own violin. It was only one-sixteenth the size of a regular violin.

Midori's mother encouraged her daughter's early interest in playing the violin.

Developing Skills

After giving Midori her first violin, Setsu began to teach her daughter how to play. Midori does not remember her early lessons. "I guess it was like learning to talk; it was a natural thing."

Midori's mother used the Suzuki method to teach Midori to play. People who use this method believe that children learn music the same way they learn to talk—without textbooks or classrooms. They think that formal teaching is not necessary to learn to play music.

Midori is often praised for her bold approach to the music she plays.

Midori gave her first public concert when she was only six years old. She loved to play the violin, and she practiced every day. She practiced for hours without any reminder from her mother. The only time Midori missed her daily violin practice was when she came down with **pneumonia** for two weeks. In the hospital, she listened to tapes so she could stay in touch with music. It took her two months to get back to playing because her hands were so swollen after her sickness.

During these years, Midori's mother continued to take her to rehearsals. While Setsu played onstage, Midori practiced in an empty room.

When Midori was eight, an American friend heard her play and was amazed by her talent. The friend recorded Midori playing and took the tape to Dorothy DeLay, a famous violin teacher at the Juilliard School of Music in New York City. The sound on this homemade recording was very poor. Dogs could be heard barking in the background. Nevertheless, DeLay was very impressed with Midori's skill, and she invited Midori to play at the Aspen Music Festival in 1981. This festival was Midori's American **debut**.

The famous violinist Pinchas Zukerman heard Midori play at the festival. He, too, thought she was a great violinist. Zukerman was so moved by her playing that he sat still throughout her performance with tears running down his cheeks. He later turned to the audience and said, "Ladies and gentlemen, I don't know about you, but I've just witnessed a miracle."

BACKGROUNDER

The Juilliard School of Music

The Juilliard School of Music is the leading school for the performing arts in the United States. Students can study music, dance, and drama. The Institute of Musical Art was founded in 1905 by Dr. Frank Damrosch. His goal was to build a school that would be as good as the classical music schools that had existed in Europe for centuries. In 1919, a wealthy merchant left $20 million in his will for musical education in New York City. The trustees used the money to set up the Juilliard Graduate School. In 1946, the two schools joined together and are now known as the Juilliard School of Music.

Midori, at the age of ten, was able to play more music than many musicians twice her age.

Accomplishments

After her first trip to the United States, Midori and her mother moved to New York City so Midori could go to the Juilliard School. She had been given a full scholarship. This was a hard time for Midori. She had to adjust to a new country, and her parents' divorce. Her music helped her through the changes in her life.

While Midori was attending the Juilliard School, the music director of the New York Philharmonic Orchestra heard her play. He invited her to be the special guest at the orchestra's New Year's Eve concert. She was eleven years old. That night, Midori received a standing **ovation** for her performance. This was only the first of many standing ovations Midori would receive.

While studying music at the Juilliard School, Midori kept up with her schoolwork even when she was on tour. In 1985, Midori went to Toronto to make her Canadian debut. Two months later, she returned to Japan to play in a special concert marking the fortieth anniversary of the bombing of Hiroshima, Japan, during World War II.

By 1990, Midori was performing up to ninety concerts a year. Even while traveling, Midori practiced three to four hours each day and spent another two or three hours on schoolwork.

Midori was fourteen when she made her famous appearance at the Tanglewood Music Festival in Massachusetts. She was playing a very difficult piece of music, and one of the strings on her violin broke. Midori calmly put her violin down and borrowed a violin from the concertmaster. A string broke on this violin as well. Without getting frightened or worried, Midori borrowed a second violin and finished her performance without a single mistake. When the piece was over, the audience, the orchestra, and the composer all gave Midori a standing ovation. They cheered, stomped their feet, and whistled. Midori was surprised by people's reaction. As she later explained, "I didn't want to stop. I love that piece."

At fifteen, Midori left the Juilliard School and has been performing all over the world ever since. In 1987, she made her debut with the London Symphony in England. In 1990, on her eighteenth birthday, she made her New York recital debut at Carnegie Hall before a sold-out audience.

Some people worried that Midori, like other child **prodigies**, would not develop into a mature musician. However, Midori continues to improve and to impress music lovers all over the world.

Quick Notes

- Midori studies karate, writes short stories, and reads in her spare time.

- Midori speaks English perfectly and is now a bit uncomfortable speaking her first language, Japanese.

- Midori writes a regular column about life in the United States for a Japanese teen magazine.

- Midori has appeared on television many times, including a program for the 1992 Olympic Winter Games and "Sesame Street."

Leonard Bernstein and the orchestra applauded Midori after her performance at the Tanglewood Music Festival in 1986. Midori's Tanglewood performance was reported on the front page of The New York Times.

"I feel so comfortable on stage; I feel safest."

"I do think that children ought to be told not only that they are loved, but also that they are attractive or at least made to feel they are."

Mary O'Hara

Irish Harpist and Singer

Early Years

Born in County Sligo on the western coast of Ireland, Mary was the youngest of four children. Mary did not enjoy her childhood. Her mother was often unhappy, and her parents had a difficult marriage. Her mother often threatened to leave the family.

Mary believed that Joan, her oldest sister, was the only child her mother really wanted. Her mother once told Mary that she had been a thin baby. She had been ashamed to show Mary to her friends. This comment began Mary's childhood worry about how she looked. She thought of herself as an ugly duckling. However, Mary did remember some happy times. Her father loved to tell jokes, and her mother played the piano and sang to Mary and her **siblings**.

Developing Skills

Mary's mother quickly realized that her young daughter could sing well. She entered Mary in singing contests at local festivals. Mary did not enjoy performing in public. But much to her surprise, she would often win.

Mary went to a boarding school where she took singing and piano lessons. One year, the school put on a play. Since Mary was such a talented singer, the teachers chose her, along with two other girls, to learn to play the small knee harp. When the play was over, Mary continued taking lessons.

Mary was paid £2.00 per song for her first radio performances. At the time, she was making good money for a young woman in Ireland.

As the years passed, Mary lost interest in school. She did not like any of her subjects, and she did not know what she wanted to do when she finished school.

Her mother advised Mary to practice the harp, and her sister Joan encouraged her to keep singing. Joan was an actress in Dublin, and she got Mary a few jobs on the radio, singing and playing the harp. At sixteen, Mary performed on her first radio program.

"Without having to seek it, a fairly steady flow of work was coming in."

On Saturdays, Mary took lessons at the Irish Academy of Music. Here she learned many of the traditional Irish songs for which she is now famous. She also took extra lessons on the concert harp.

Around this time, Mary got her own radio show called "Children at the Mike." It was a fifteen-minute program where she played and sang traditional Irish songs.

In 1954, Mary took a short break from her life in Ireland and went to stay with her father. He had been posted with the army on the west coast of Africa. Mary enjoyed the time with her father, and she even did a little performing. She gave a recital and sang and played the harp on the radio.

Mary returned to Ireland in the winter. She continued her routine of singing and playing the harp on the radio and in small recitals.

In the summer of 1955, Mary met her future husband, Richard Selig. He was an American poet who was studying at Oxford University in England.

BACKGROUNDER

The Harp

The harp is one of the oldest instruments still used today. Drawings from the pyramids show that there were harps in Ancient Egypt—as far back as 4,500 years ago. In Europe, the harp first appeared in Ireland in the eighth century. It is now one of the country's national symbols. The modern concert harp is the one that is most used today. It is 70 inches tall (178 centimeters), with forty-seven strings and seven foot pedals.

Mary's lessons at the Irish Academy were free and open to anyone who wanted to attend. The instructor taught by singing one phrase at a time which his students would then repeat.

Quick Notes

- In 1978, Mary appeared on the television show "This Is Your Life."

- Mary always gets nervous before going on stage. She compares walking onto the stage to walking on a tightrope.

> "I mean no disrespect to other ... talented performers when I say that the response to Mary O'Hara was unique."
>
> Russell Harty

Accomplishments

Life was going for well for Mary. She had fallen in love with Richard, and she was invited to perform at the Edinburgh Festival in Scotland. She had also started to record albums, and she appeared on television for the first time. Shortly after this appearance, Mary got an agent. By the age of twenty, Mary had her own television program on Saturday nights and later her own children's show.

On July 23, 1956, Mary and Richard were married. Even though Mary's music was best-known in Ireland, Scotland, and England, the couple decided to move to the United States.

Life in the United States was not easy. Richard was told he had a type of cancer called **Hodgkin's disease**. When he became too weak to work, Mary decided to earn money by singing and playing the harp again.

With the money her father had given them for a wedding present, Mary bought a concert harp and took a few lessons. Mary made a second and then a third album. Soon after she finished her third album, Richard died. Mary believed she would never record music again. She said her "interest in singing had died with him."

Mary performed at the Edinburgh Festival in 1956 as part of an event called The Pleasures of Scotland.

The night Richard died, Mary decided to end her singing career and enter a **monastery**. She returned to Ireland to search for a monastery that would accept her. In the meantime, she earned her living by singing and playing her harp. She toured, gave recitals and concerts, and she recorded songs that were later made into four albums. In April 1962, Mary entered the Stanbrook monastery in England, where she lived and worked as Sister Miriam.

Mary planned to stay in Stanbrook for the rest of her life. She loved being at the monastery, but she began to get sick. Her doctor advised her to leave. In 1974, she left Stanbrook after twelve years.

Mary found it hard at first to adjust to life outside the monastery. However, after an appearance on television, Mary became more encouraged. Strangers approached her on the street and told her how glad they were that she was back. After twelve years away, she was still as popular as ever.

BACKGROUNDER

A Memorable Performance

Shortly after leaving the monastery, Mary appeared on "The Russell Harty Show" in London, England. During the rehearsal, she sang a traditional Gaelic song. It was so beautiful that everyone in the studio stopped what they were doing. When Mary finished, they all cheered. She sang the same song on air that night. The next day, the radio station was flooded with calls from Mary's fans. She was asked to return to the show the next week—something that had never been done before.

Before he died, Richard had asked Mary to promise to marry again. In 1985, twenty-eight years after Richard's death, Mary married Dr. Paidrig O'Toole.

"It is your music that cured me forever of the old delusions that women could not do men's work in art and other things."

George Bernard Shaw

Ethel Smyth

British Composer

Early Years

Ethel grew up in a well-to-do family with seven brothers and sisters. It was a strict household run by her father, a general with the British military. This did not stop young Ethel from getting into trouble. She and her sister were sometimes sent to the attic when they misbehaved. One of Ethel's nannies once asked her, "You have a very strong will; why not the will to be good?"

Although her mother played the piano and sang very well, Ethel did not show any interest in music until she was twelve. Then the Smyths hired a new **governess**. She had studied music at the famous Leipzig Conservatory in Germany, one of the best music schools in Europe. The governess taught Ethel to play the piano.

BACKGROUNDER

The Leipzig Conservatory

The city of Leipzig is important in the history of music. The Conservatory, or music school, was founded in 1843 by Felix Mendelssohn. Felix and his sister Fanny were both famous composers. During the 1800s, many of Europe's greatest musicians performed in the city. Composers such as Johannes Brahms and Robert and Clara Schumann lived in Leipzig during this time.

Composer Fanny Mendelssohn first published her music under her brother's name because many publishers would not accept music composed by a woman.

Developing Skills

Soon, Ethel became a good piano player and singer. But Ethel did not want to perform. She wanted to compose, and she began to write short pieces of music.

Ethel did not begin her formal musical training until she was seventeen years old. She borrowed a book written by the composer Hector Berlioz called *Treatise on Instrumentation*. With this book, Ethel taught herself how to write music for all the instruments in an orchestra. She hired a teacher and took private music lessons. However, Ethel's father did not support her interest in music, and he fired the teacher.

Ethel had a strong will and was not going to let her father stop her from becoming a composer. One night, while the family was having dinner, Ethel made an announcement. She said that she was going to Germany to study at the Leipzig Conservatory. She said that she would run away from home and starve once she got there if necessary. Her father did not like the idea of his daughter becoming a musician. He told Ethel he would rather see her "under the sod" than a musician.

Ethel's inheritance gave her enough money to pursue her dream of becoming a composer.

Ethel was as stubborn as her father. She tried to make life at home so difficult that he would give in and let her go to Germany. She stopped going to church. She refused to sing at the Smyths' parties, and finally she stopped speaking to anyone. Ethel sneaked off to concerts, borrowing money from store-owners in the village. She told them her father would pay them back.

By the time Ethel was nineteen, her father gave up and let her go to Germany. He thought she would soon return home. She left for the Leipzig Conservatory in 1877 with her brother-in-law as a **chaperone**.

Ethel took courses in composition, **counterpoint**, and the piano. But she was disappointed with the conservatory. She thought the teachers were dull and her fellow students were not as interested in music as she was. She began to compose songs on her own. After a year, she quit school and hired a private tutor to teach her composition. Her teacher was Heinrich von Herzogenberg, an Austrian composer. He and his wife became close friends with Ethel and introduced her to other musicians.

"The whole English attitude towards women in the fields of art is ludicrous and uncivilized.... How you play the violin, paint, or compose is what matters."

Quick Notes

- **Ethel began writing books when she was sixty years old. She published ten books. Four were autobiographies.**

- **Ethel's opera *Der Wald* was the first opera composed by a woman to be performed at the Metropolitan Opera House in New York City. It was performed there in 1903.**

- **A series of concerts was performed in London in honor of Ethel's seventy-fifth birthday. Although she sat proudly through them, she could not hear anything. She had gone deaf.**

Accomplishments

In 1878, Ethel took the pieces she had composed to a music publishing house in Germany. At first, the publisher refused them. He said that pieces composed by women did not sell well. But Ethel was determined and made him listen to her songs. After hearing her music, he said he would take a risk and publish it. Ethel was so happy that she said she would not take any money.

Ethel continued to study composition. By 1890, she had written her first piece for an orchestra. It was called *Serenade,* and it was performed for the first time at the Crystal Palace in London. She was inspired by the success of *Serenade* to write *Antony and Cleopatra* which was performed six months later. Ethel was just thirty-three years old.

Ethel loved hats. She was often seen in a three-cornered hat that was one of her favorites.

"The people who have helped me most at difficult moments of my musical career … have been members of my own sex."

Ethel continued to compose, and by 1891, she had written *Mass in D* for orchestra and **chorus**. Ethel was very excited about her new piece. People compared it to the work of Beethoven and Bach, two of the world's greatest composers.

When Ethel played *Mass in D* for the German conductor Hermann Levi, he was so impressed that he told Ethel to "sit down at once and write an opera." Ethel took the challenge.

A few years before, Ethel had fallen in love with Henry Brewster, an American living in Germany. He helped her write her operas. He wrote the words, and she composed the music. Because few operas were being performed in England, Henry wrote them in German. Ethel's first two operas, *Fantasio* (Fantasy) and *Der Wald* (The Forest), were very successful in Germany. Ethel traveled with them to England and then to the United States. Ethel's third opera, *The Wreckers*, is thought by many to be her greatest work.

Ethel wrote many more operas and orchestral pieces. Although they were all popular, Ethel was never satisfied with the recognition given to her work. She always hoped that her true fame might come after her death.

BACKGROUNDER

The Suffragist Movement

Between 1910 and 1912, Ethel put her composing career on hold. She had decided to work for the **suffragist** movement. Up to and during most of Ethel's lifetime, women were not allowed to vote. Suffragists campaigned for the right for women to vote. During a suffragist rally, Ethel threw a rock at a government official's window. She was arrested and sentenced to two months in jail. Once Ethel was released, she returned to composing.

Before 1928, women in England did not have the right to vote. Suffragists worked to get them that right.

"I've always felt that good music, if it is well played, will touch anyone anywhere."

Vanessa-Mae

British Violinist

Early Years

Vanessa-Mae was born in Singapore, a small country in Southeast Asia. Her mother was Chinese, and her father was from Thailand. At the age of four, Vanessa-Mae moved to London, England, with her mother and stepfather. Her full name is Vanessa-Mae Vanakorn Nicholson.

As a young child, Vanessa-Mae was already a talented musician. She took her first piano lesson when she was three years old and her first violin lesson when she was five. When she was a little girl, Vanessa-Mae loved her violin as much as other children love a pet or a doll.

Backgrounder

Singapore

Singapore is at the tip of the Malay Peninsula where the South China Sea meets the Indian Ocean. Singapore has one large island and a number of smaller islands. Almost all of the people in Singapore live in the capital city that is also called Singapore. The country is very small. It is only 221 square miles (572 square kilometers).

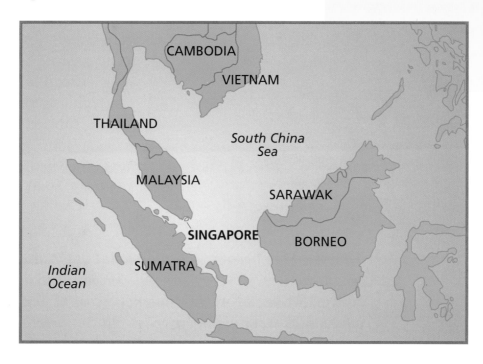

Developing Skills

Vanessa-Mae studied music at the Central Conservatory of China in Beijing. She was the youngest student the Conservatory had ever accepted. She also took lessons at the famous Royal College of Music in London. The director of the college described Vanessa-Mae as "a true child **prodigy**—like Mozart and Mendelssohn."

When Vanessa-Mae was just eight years old, she had to make a big decision. She was equally gifted at both the violin and the piano, but she had to concentrate on just one instrument. Although she had just won a prize at the British Young Pianist of the Year Competition, Vanessa-Mae chose the violin.

At the age of nine, Vanessa-Mae went to Germany to take violin classes for advanced students. The best students were chosen for a series of recitals. Most of the students were chosen to be a part of the recitals only once or twice. Vanessa-Mae was chosen four times. These were her first performances in front of an audience.

Vanessa-Mae became a professional musician when she was eleven years old. She went to a college for senior music students. Most of her classmates were eighteen years old.

By the time she was ten years old, Vanessa-Mae had studied the violin at some of the best schools in the world. She made her first professional appearance in 1987 with the Philharmonia Orchestra in London.

Vanessa-Mae often played Mozart concertos. A concerto is a piece of music written for one or more **solo** instruments accompanied by an orchestra. It was not long until she was writing her own pieces of music to include with the concertos. At a Children's Royal Variety Performance, Vanessa-Mae played her own arrangement of the song "Over the Rainbow."

BACKGROUNDER

Mozart

Wolfgang Amadeus Mozart is one of the world's greatest composers. He was born in 1756 in Salzburg, Austria, and was considered to be a child prodigy. He learned to play the **harpsichord** at the age of three. He was composing music by the time he was five, and he played for Austrian royalty at the age of six. Although he only lived to be thirty-six, he wrote over six hundred compositions. Mozart's music is enjoyed throughout the world. His hometown of Salzburg holds a music festival each summer where his music is played by many performers.

Like other talented performers, Vanessa-Mae loves to experiment with different styles of music.

"Music with its beauty, strength, and mystique is for enjoying and for playing."

Accomplishments

By the time she was twelve, Vanessa-Mae had played with orchestras all over the world as a soloist. She had also released three classical recordings. Tchaikovsky and Beethoven are two famous composers who wrote several pieces of music that are very difficult to play. Vanessa-Mae is the youngest person in the world to record violin concertos written by these two composers.

Although she loved classical music, Vanessa-Mae wanted to experiment with other kinds of music. At fourteen, she began to combine the traditional sound of her **acoustic** violin with the sounds made from her new electric violin. She called this music "techno-acoustic fusion." Vanessa-Mae loved the music that the two types of violins made together. She said it was as exciting to mix her violin solos with computer music as it was with the music of live musicians. Her first album that recorded this kind of music was called *The Violin Player*. It was an instant success and sold in over twenty countries. It was even a hit on the best-selling dance music charts.

The Violin Player *was recorded when Vanessa-Mae was only fifteen years old.*

No longer just a classical musician, Vanessa-Mae was asked to perform at international rock concerts. At a concert in Switzerland, the audience of fifty thousand people gave Vanessa-Mae a twenty-minute **ovation**. At a concert broadcast live on television in Poland, she was brought back on stage for so many **encore** performances that the national television news had to be delayed. The crowd did not want her to stop playing.

Vanessa-Mae is always looking for new experiences. The final concert of her 1997 world tour was held on a frozen lake in St. Moritz, Switzerland. Vanessa-Mae hang-glided to the stage from a spot 1.5 miles (2.4 kilometers) above the lake. With the help of a co-pilot, she glided down over the heads of the audience and landed on skis in front of the stage.

Vanessa-Mae has sometimes been criticized for not sticking only to classical music. However, Vanessa-Mae feels it is important to introduce violin music to a new audience. She is happy with her role in music today: "If as a result [of my music], people see the violin as a fresh, trendy, up-to-date instrument, that's fine with me."

"Beethoven and Beatles, Mozart and Michael Jackson, Paganini and Prince—I like them all."

Quick Notes

- **Vanessa-Mae was the youngest speaker ever to address the Oxford University Union in its 172-year history.**

- **Being a little superstitious, Vanessa-Mae walks over freshly spilled water between her dressing room and the stage before every performance. She believes it brings her good luck.**

- **Vanessa-Mae loves animals and has four dogs and a bird.**

Key Events

1916 Performs for the first time at age six

1922 Begins her professional career

1926 Marries John Williams

1927 Moves to Memphis, Tennessee, with the Seymour and Jeanette Show

1929 Joins Andy Kirk and the Twelve Clouds of Joy

1929 Moves with the Kirk band to Kansas City

1942 Moves to New York City

1945 Begins her own radio show called the "Mary Lou Williams Piano Workshop"

1952 Moves to Europe

1954 Returns to the United States and retires from playing music

1956 Comes out of retirement

1977 Begins teaching at Duke University

"I think that if a woman has something to do, she should just do it."

Mary Lou Williams

American Jazz Pianist

Early Years

When Mary Lou was a baby, her mother played **ragtime** and spiritual music on the piano with Mary Lou on her lap. Mary Lou began to play the piano when she was two years old. One day, while sitting on her mother's lap, Mary Lou's hands beat her mother's to the keyboard. She began to play before her mother got the chance. Mary Lou said, "It must have been pretty good because she dropped me and she went to get the neighbors to listen."

At age four, Mary Lou moved with her mother and sister from Atlanta to Pittsburgh, Pennsylvania. Her stepfather bought her a player piano and took her to bars where she learned to play ragtime, blues, and **boogie woogie** music.

BACKGROUNDER

Player Pianos

A player piano has special machinery for playing music automatically. It has a roll of paper with patterns of holes. These holes help make different notes. The paper roll moves over a metal roll underneath that also has small holes. Inside the metal roll there is a pump that acts like a vacuum. As the air is sucked through the holes, the pressure forces small pieces of wood inside the piano to strike the strings. When the keys are struck they produce music. Player pianos were very popular during the late 1800s and early 1900s.

*At age six, Mary Lou made her piano **debut** at a picnic. Before long, word about Mary Lou's talent spread. By the age of ten, she was known around Pittsburgh as the "Little Piano Girl."*

Developing Skills

Mary Lou's mother had taken formal classes in music and piano. She did not want Mary Lou to learn this way because she thought people should learn first by ear. She encouraged Mary Lou to play the music she heard and liked. This way of learning affected Mary Lou's playing for the rest of her life. She felt that because she learned to play on her own, rather than with formal teachers, she had a stronger and deeper feeling toward music.

Music was everywhere in Mary Lou's early years. Her mother brought professional musicians home to play for Mary Lou. Her stepfather bought her piano scrolls for her player piano. Her uncle encouraged her to play Irish songs, and her grandfather urged her to play classical music.

"You can't teach jazz out of books. You got to teach the student to teach himself. You got to teach him how to listen."

Mary Lou developed quickly as a musician. Many people in Pittsburgh began to hear of the Little Piano Girl. Some of the richest families in the city sent their limousines to pick her up so she could play at their parties.

Her brother-in-law, Hugh, took Mary Lou to theaters and music halls. There, Mary Lou heard the great popular musicians, such as blues queen Ma Rainey, perform. Soon, Mary Lou was playing professionally with local bands. In 1922, when she was just twelve years old, Mary Lou filled in for a pianist in the Buzz and Harris Revue, a theater show that was visiting Pittsburgh. Mary Lou played so well that her parents allowed her go on tour with the group for two weeks.

For the next few years, while still at high school, Mary Lou went on tour with a number of other groups. One group was the Seymour and Jeanette Show, an African-American vaudeville troop. In 1926, when she was sixteen, Mary Lou married John Williams, the saxophone player and leader of the Show's band. The couple settled with the Show in Memphis, Tennessee.

BACKGROUNDER

Vaudeville

Vaudeville is a kind of entertainment that features a variety of acts, such as juggling, singing, dancing, and skits. It was the most popular form of theater in the United States from the 1880s to the 1930s. Vaudeville theaters were found across the country. Different acts traveled around to each of the theaters. Most vaudeville performances had eight to ten different acts. In the 1920s, people lost interest in vaudeville because of the popularity of motion pictures, or movies.

Mary Lou liked to play with other women musicians. She held informal practices in her apartment to encourage women musicians to work together.

Kansas City Big Band Style Jazz

Jazz music became very popular in the 1920s in Kansas City. Because it was an important depot for buses and trains, all the musicians traveling to the West or East had to pass through Kansas City. It soon became a town of dance halls and nightclubs. The area that attracted most of the big-name musicians, 18th and Vine, was the city's music center. Musicians from across the country got together to play, and they developed a new style of jazz—the big band sound.

Accomplishments

In 1927, while Mary Lou was in Memphis, she made her first recordings with two popular jazz groups. John moved to Oklahoma City to join a band known as Andy Kirk and the Twelve Clouds of Joy. Mary Lou soon joined her husband and the new band.

She served as their pianist, their part-time chauffeur, and she began her career as a music arranger. Arrangers adapt pieces of music so they can be played by different instruments.

At the end of 1929, the Kirk band moved to Kansas City and quickly became one of the most popular bands of the region. With the Kirk band, Mary Lou became well known across the country as both an outstanding pianist and one of the best arrangers in the business. She wrote arrangements for some of the most famous jazz performers of the time, such as Louis Armstrong, Duke Ellington, and Benny Goodman.

In 1942, Mary Lou moved to New York City and formed a band with her second husband, trumpeter Harold Baker. This marriage did not last long, but Mary Lou stayed on in New York City.

Mary Lou stayed in Kansas City for thirteen years. She became known as the "First Lady of Jazz."

During this time, Mary Lou worked with young musicians who had developed another new style of jazz. These **bebop** musicians included players such as Charlie Parker and Miles Davis. Mary Lou's apartment in Harlem was a center for the young musicians to come together and play. During most of the 1940s and 1950s, Mary Lou was the only female musician who was considered an equal to the great jazzmen of the time.

In 1952, Mary Lou went to Europe to play a couple of shows. She stayed two years. Then one night in 1954, she "stopped playing and started praying," according to Mary Lou. She began to devote her life to religion and helping young people and musicians in need. She did not play for three years. Finally, trumpeter Dizzy Gillespie persuaded her to play with him at the Newport Jazz Festival. From then on, Mary Lou combined her love for music with her religious faith. She composed religious pieces for jazz groups and orchestras. She began to teach, and from 1977 until her death in 1981, Mary Lou Williams was one of the most respected teachers at Duke University in North Carolina.

Quick Notes

- Mary was the first woman to establish her own record company. It was called Mary Records.

- In 1956, Mary opened two thrift shops in New York for needy musicians.

- When Mary began teaching music at Duke University in Durham, North Carolina, the sale of jazz albums went up in the city by forty percent.

- A documentary on the life of Mary Lou Williams was filmed in 1990. It is called *Music on My Mind*.

"If you're going to get something done, you can never take no for an answer, and you got to do it yourself."

More Women in Profile

There are many more women around the world who are wonderful musicians than can be listed in one book. Here are a few more you can read about. Use the Suggested Reading list to learn more about these and other women musicians.

1898–1971

Lillian "Lil" Hardin Armstrong

American Jazz Pianist

"I was born to swing, that's all."

Lil began her musical life as the pianist and organist in her school and church in Memphis, Tennessee. She continued playing the piano until the day she died. She performed with some of the best jazz musicians of the day, at a time when piano players were a central part of every band. Lil died on stage while performing in a memorial concert for Louis Armstrong, her ex-husband.

1959–

Cindy Blackman

American Drummer

Cindy comes from a family of musicians. As a child in Yellow Springs, Ohio, she loved to play the drums and begged her parents to buy her a drum set. Finally, they gave in. After finishing high school, Cindy studied music at the University of Connecticut. She quickly became bored and moved to New York City where she could learn music first

hand. She played in jazz clubs and soon began making her own recordings. In 1993, she toured with Lenny Kravitz's rock band. Cindy's lively style has made her popular with music fans everywhere.

Cindy Blackman

1955–

Jane Ira Bloom

American Saxophonist

Jane learned to play the saxophone as a child in Massachusetts. She studied music and composition at Yale University for five years. After earning her bachelor's and master's degrees in music, she moved to New York City. She believes that great saxophonists do not just play their instrument. They get it to "sing."

1951–

Laurie Frink

American Trumpeter

"Music has no gender."

Laurie is a lead trumpeter—the player who not only leads the trumpet section but the entire band as well. She began training in classical music at the age of ten, but switched to jazz in her twenties in New York City. Despite her talent, she does not always find it easy to compete with men. She believes women still do not have the same opportunities as men in the world of music. A friend of Laurie's, a trumpet player, was turned down for a job when the conductor said, "I want a man in that chair."

1956–

Sharon Isbin

American Guitarist

When Sharon was young, she wanted to be a scientist like her father. But when she was nine, while her family was living in Italy, she learned how to play the guitar. She is now one of the best guitarists in the world. She can play many kinds of music, including Spanish, jazz, and modern songs. She began touring Europe each year when she was seventeen years old and has been playing all over the world since then. In 1989, she became the Juilliard School of Music's first guitar instructor.

1965–

Ofra Harnoy

Canadian Cellist

Ofra was born in Israel but grew up in Canada. By the time she was ten, Ofra had played with both the Toronto and Montréal Symphony Orchestras. In 1992, she was the youngest person to win the International Concert Artists Guild Award. Ofra tries to reach as many people as possible through her music. She hopes to interest young audiences in classical music. She has performed in Asia, the Middle East, and North America.

Ofra Harnoy

1879–1959

Wanda Landowska

Polish Harpsichordist

Born in Warsaw, Poland, Wanda is considered a legend in the history of music. In 1925, she founded a music school in France. It was for people who wanted to learn to play instruments that were seldom used. Wanda herself played the **harpsichord**, an instrument that was invented in the fourteenth century and is similar to the piano. She is also remembered for her lectures and studies on many of the world's greatest composers. Many believe she was a musical genius.

1972–

Natalie MacMaster

Canadian Fiddler

Natalie was brought up in a musical family on Cape Breton Island, Canada. Her family has many connections to their Scottish ancestors, especially to Scottish-Celtic music. Natalie was given her first fiddle and lessons by her great uncle, Buddy. He was a master of the fiddle. Natalie's lively style is loved by audiences everywhere. She dances and plays her fiddle with passion. In 1995, when performing in Chattanooga, Tennessee, Natalie broke all but her two bottom fiddle strings. Audiences were impressed when she continued playing and finished her performance.

1903–1983

Frédérique Petrides

Belgian Conductor and Publisher

Frédérique Petrides devoted her life to helping women become more accepted as musicians. She moved from Belgium to the United States in 1923. She wanted to conduct an orchestra, but in the 1930s, women were not allowed to conduct important orchestras. So in 1933, Frédérique founded her own women's orchestra— the Orchestrette of New York. It was a success. In the twelve years she conducted the Orchestrette, it grew from fourteen to thirty-five women. She also published a magazine called *Women in Music*. It was about female musicians, and it encouraged women to be more active in the world of music.

Natalie MacMaster

1914–

Rosalyn Tureck

American Concert Artist, Conductor, and Educator

As a child growing up in Chicago, Illinois, Rosalyn began to imitate what her older sister was learning in her piano lessons. When Rosalyn was only twelve years old, she played with the Chicago Symphony Orchestra. She not only plays the piano, but has also performed as a soloist on the **harpsichord**, organ, and **clavichord**. She became an expert in the music of Johann Sebastian Bach, a famous composer. In 1958, she was the first woman to conduct the New York Philharmonic Orchestra. Rosalyn encouraged young composers and performers. She held annual concerts in her New York apartment that showcased new talent. Invitations to these private concerts were prized by music fans from all over North America and Europe. In addition to performing and conducting, Rosalyn has taught music at several universities in the United States, Canada, and England.

1962–

Rachel Z

American Jazz Pianist

Born in New York City as Rachel Nicolazzo, Rachel was expected to become an opera singer like her mother. Rachel began taking voice lessons at the age of two and piano lessons at age seven. She first heard jazz musician Herbie Hancock's music when she was at a summer music school. She decided then that she would be a jazz musician. Rachel has been inspired by the work of other women artists and musicians. On her album, *Room of One's Own*, each song is dedicated to a female artist who has influenced Rachel's life and work.

Rachel Z

Glossary

acoustic: a type of instrument that does not amplify its sound electrically

autobiography: a story written by a person about his or her own life

bebop: a fast-paced style of jazz developed in the 1940s

boogie woogie: a style of jazz that is usually played on the piano

chaperone: an older person who accompanies a younger person to protect them and ensure they behave properly

chorus: a group of people who sing together

clavichord: an early musical instrument with both strings and a keyboard

counterpoint: combining two or more melodies in harmony

debut: a first public appearance

drought: a period of continuous dry weather

encore: a repeat performance

governess: a woman who is employed to teach children in their home

harpsichord: a musical instrument with a keyboard like a piano

Hodgkin's disease: a disease that causes the lymph nodes, spleen, and liver to enlarge

monastery: a place where people who are part of a religious community live and work

ovation: enthusiastic applause

pneumonia: a disease of the lungs

prodigy: a person who is remarkably talented in some area

ragtime: an early style of jazz performed mostly on the piano

recorder: a flute with a mouth piece like a whistle

sibling: a brother or sister

solo: by oneself

suffragist: a person who wants women to have the right to vote

Suggested Reading

Bowers, Jand and Judith Tick. *Women Making Music: The Western Art Tradition, 1150–1950*. Chicago: University of Illinois Press, 1986.

Dahl, Linda. *Stormy Weather: The Music and Lives of a Century of Jazzwomen*. New York: Pantheon Books, 1984.

Groh, Jan Bell. *Evening the Score*. Fayetteville: University of Arkansas Press, 1991.

Hacker, Carlotta. *Great African Americans in Jazz*. Niagara-on-the-Lake: Crabtree Publishing, 1997.

Lees, Gene. *Jazz Lives: 100 Portraits in Jazz*. Buffalo: Firefly Books, 1992.

Lyons, Len. *The Great Jazz Pianists: Speaking of Their Lives and Music*. New York: William Morrow and Company, Inc., 1983.

Nichols, Janet. *Women Music Makers: An Introduction to Women Composers*. New York: Walker and Company, 1992.

O'Hara, Mary. *The Scent of the Roses*. London: Michael Joseph, 1980.

Smittroh, Linda and Mary Reilly McCall. *Women's Almanac, Volume 3*. Detroit: UXL, 1997.

Index

1 2 3 4 5 6 7 8 9 0 Printed in Canada 7 6 5 4 3 2 1 0 9 8